Dear Marlene,

Just a small token
to help you pass your
time pleasantly and lift
your spirits.

Ellie Whitbloom

Gift From the Sea

Selections

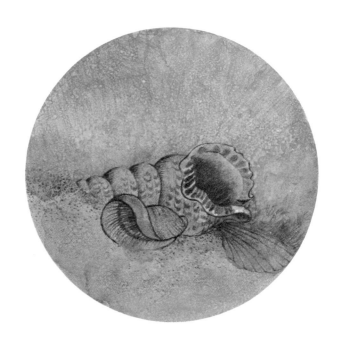

Anne Morrow Lindbergh

Selections From Gift From the Sea

Illustrations by Bill Greer

HALLMARK EDITIONS

I began these pages for myself, in order to think out my own particular pattern of living, my own individual balance of life, work and human relationships. And since I think best with a pencil in my hand, I started naturally to write. . . . Gradually, these chapters, fed by conversations, arguments and revelations from men and women of all groups, became more than my individual story, until I decided in the end to give them back to the people who had shared and stimulated many of these thoughts. Here, then, with my warm feelings of gratitude and companionship for those working along the same lines, I return my gift from the sea.

The shell in my hand is deserted. It once housed a whelk, a snail-like creature, and then, after the death of the first occupant, a little hermit crab, who has run away, leaving his tracks behind him.

Why did he run away? Did he hope to find a better home, a better mode of living? I too have run away, I realize, I have shed the shell of my life, for these few weeks of vacation.

But his shell—it is simple; it is bare, it is beautiful. My shell is not like this. How untidy it has become! Blurred with moss, knobby with barnacles, its shape is hardly recognizable anymore. Surely, it had a shape once. What is the shape of my life?

The shape of my life is determined by many things; my background and childhood, my mind and education, my conscience and its pressures, my heart and its desires. I want to give and take from my children and husband, to share with friends and community, to carry out my obligations as a woman, as an artist, as a citizen.

But I want first of all to be at peace with myself. I want a singleness of eye, a purity of intention, a central core to my life that will enable me to carry out these obligations as well as I can. I would like to achieve a state of spiritual grace from which I could function and give as I was meant to in the eye of God.

There are techniques in the search for grace. And techniques can be cultivated. I have learned by some experience, by many examples, and by the writings of others before me, also occupied in the search for grace, that there are, in fact, certain roads that one may follow. Simplification of life is one of them.

I mean to lead a simple life, to choose a simple shell I can carry easily—like a hermit crab. But I do not. I find that my frame of life does not foster simplicity. The life I have chosen as wife and mother entrains a whole caravan of complications. It involves a house, food and shelter, meals, planning, marketing, bills, and making ends meet. It involves health, education, clothes, shopping, laundry, cleaning; it involves friends, my husband's, my children's, my own, and endless arrangements to get together.

Life today in America is based on ever-widen-

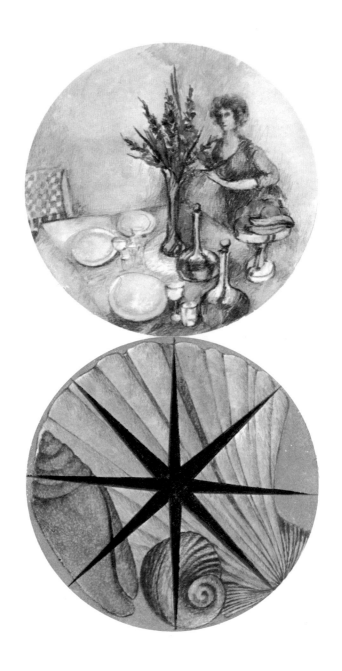

ing circles of contact and communication. It involves not only family demands, but community demands, national and international demands, through social and cultural pressures, through the mass media.

My mind reels with it. What a circus act we women perform every day of our lives. This is not the life of simplicity but the life of multiplicity that wise men warn us of. It leads not to unification but to fragmentation. It does not bring grace; it destroys the soul.

The problem of multiplicity of life not only confronts the American woman, but also the American man. And it is not limited to our present civilization; it has always been one of the pitfalls of mankind. Yet, the problem is particularly and essentially woman's.

To be a woman is to have interests and duties raying out in all directions; the pattern of our lives is circular. We must be open to all points of the compass: husband, children, friends, home, community. How difficult for us, then, to achieve a balance in the midst of these contradictory tensions, and yet how necessary for the proper functioning of our lives.

With a new awareness, I begin to understand why the saints were rarely married women. It has to do primarily with distractions. The bearing and rearing of children, the running of a house, human relationships with their myriad pulls—woman's normal occupations run counter to creative life, or contemplative life, or saintly life. The problem is not merely one of Woman and the Home or Woman and Career, but more basically: how to remain whole in the midst of the distractions of life.

What is the answer? I have only clues, shells from the sea. The bare beauty of the channelled whelk tells me that one answer, and perhaps a first step, is in cutting out some of the distractions. But how? I must find a balance somewhere between island solitude and communion, between retreat and return.

In my periods of retreat, perhaps I can learn something to carry back into my worldly life. I can follow this superficial clue and see where it leads. Here, in beach living, I can try.

One learns first of all in beach living the art of shedding: how little one can get along with, not how much. I find I live quite happily without those things I think necessary in winter in the North. I remember again, ironically, that today more of us in America than anywhere else in the world have the luxury of choice between simplicity and complication of life. And for the most part, we, who could choose simplicity, choose complication. The monk and the nun choose simplicity of their own free will. But if one accidentally finds it, as I have for a few days, one finds also the serenity it brings.

Is it not rather ugly, one may ask? One collects material possessions not only for security, comfort or vanity, but for beauty as well. Is your sea-shell house not ugly and bare? No, it is beautiful, my house. It is bare, of course, but the wind, the sun, the smell of the pines blow through its bareness.

I am content, I love my sea-shell of a house. I wish I could live in it always. I wish I could transport it home. But I cannot. I can only carry back my little channelled whelk. It will sit on my desk in Connecticut, to remind me of the ideal of a simplified life, to encourage me in the game I played on the beach. To ask how little, not how much, can I get along with. To say—is it necessary?—when I am tempted to add one more accumulation to my life, when I am pulled toward one more centrifugal activity.

Simplification of outward life is not enough. It is merely the outside. But I am starting with the outside. I am looking at the outside of a shell, the outside of my life—the shell. This is only a technique, a road to grace. The final answer, I know, is always inside. But the outside can give a clue, can help one to find the inside answer.

Channelled whelk, I put you down again, but you have set my mind on a journey, up an inwardly winding spiral staircase of thought.

MOON SHELL

This is a snail shell, round, full and glossy as a horse chestnut. Comfortable and compact, it sits curled up like a cat in the hollow of my hand. On its smooth symmetrical face is pencilled with precision a perfect spiral winding inward to the tiny dark core of the apex, the pupil of the eye. It stares at me, this mysterious single eye—and I stare back.

Now it is the moon, now the eye of a cat. Now it is an island, alone, self-contained, serene. How wonderful are islands! Islands in space, like this one I have come to, ringed about by miles of water, linked by no bridges, no cables, no telephones. An island from the world and the world's life.

People, too, become like islands in such an atmosphere, self-contained, whole and serene; standing back in reverence before the miracle of another individual.

We are all, in the last analysis, alone. And this basic state of solitude is not something we have any choice about. We may delude ourselves, but how much better to realize that we are so.

How one hates to think of oneself as alone.

How one avoids it. It seems to imply rejection or unpopularity. We seem so frightened today of being alone that we never let it happen.

Now, instead of planting our solitude with our own dream blossoms, we choke the space with continuous music, chatter, and companionship to which we do not even listen. It is simply there to fill a vacuum. When the noise stops there is no inner music to take its place.

It is difficult today to leave one's friends and family and deliberately practice the art of solitude for an hour or a day or a week. And yet, once it is done, I find there is a quality to being alone that is incredibly precious. Life rushes back into the void, richer, more vivid, fuller than before.

For a full day and two nights I have been alone. And it seemed to me, separated from my own species, that I was nearer to others: the shy willet; the sand piper, running in little unfrightened steps down the shining beach rim ahead of me; the old gull, hunched up, grouchy, surveying the horizon.

Yes, I felt closer to my fellow men too, even

in my solitude. For it is not physical solitude that actually separates one from other men, not physical, but spiritual isolation. When one is a stranger to oneself, one is estranged from others too. If one is out of touch with oneself,

then one cannot touch others. Only when one is connected to one's own core is one connected to others, I am beginning to discover. And for me, the core, the inner spring, can best be found through solitude.

I walked far down the beach, soothed by the rhythm of the waves, the wind and mist from the spray on my hair. And then home, full to the brim with my day alone. There is a quality to fullness that the Psalmist expressed:

"My cup runneth over." Let no one come—I pray in sudden panic—I might spill myself away!

Is this what happens to woman? She wants perpetually to spill herself away. All her instinct as a woman demands that she give. Her time, her energy, her creativeness drain out if there is any chance, any leak.

But why not, one may ask? What is wrong with woman's spilling herself away, since it is her function to give?

The artist naturally always resents giving himself in small drops, and woman instinctively wants to give, yet resents giving herself in small pieces. I believe that what woman resents is not so much giving herself in pieces as giving herself purposelessly.

We do not see the results of our giving as concretely as a man does his work. In the job of home-keeping there is no raise from the boss, and seldom praise from others to show us we have hit the mark. Except for the child, woman's creation is so often invisible, especially today. It is hard even to think of it as purposeful activity, so much of it is automatic. Woman herself begins to feel like a telephone exchange or a laundromat.

Purposeful giving is not as apt to deplete one's resources; it renews itself even in the act of depletion—like milk in the breast. But no longer fed by a feeling of indispensability or purposefulness, we are hungry, and not knowing what we are hungry for, we fill up the void with endless distractions. Hunger, of course, cannot be fed merely by a feeling of indispensability. If it is woman's function to give, she must be replenished too. But how?

Solitude, says the moon shell. Every person, especially every woman, should be alone sometime during the year, some part of each week, and each day. To many women, such a program seems quite out of reach. They have no extra income to spend on a vacation for themselves, no time left over from household drudgery, no energy after the daily cooking and cleaning for even an hour of creative solitude.

Is this then only an economic problem? I do not think so. By and large, mothers and housewives are the vacationless class. But if women were convinced that a day off or an hour of solitude was a reasonable ambition, they would find a way of attaining it.

How inexplicable it seems. Anything else

will be accepted as a better excuse. If one sets aside time for a trip to the hairdresser, a social engagement, or a shopping expedition, that time is accepted as inviolable. But if one says: I cannot come because that is my hour to be alone, one is considered rude, egotistical or strange. What a commentary on our civilization when being alone is considered suspect; when one has to apologize for it, make excuses, hide the fact that one practices it—like a secret vice!

But women need solitude in order to find the true essence of themselves. The problem is not entirely in finding a room of one's own, the time alone, difficult and necessary as this is. The problem is more how to still the soul in the midst of its activities. In fact, the problem is how to feed the soul.

It is the spirit of woman that is going dry, not the mechanics that are wanting; certainly our lives are easier, freer, more open to opportunities. But these hard-won prizes are insufficient because we have not yet learned how to use them. We are aware of our hunger and needs, but still ignorant of what will satisfy them. Not knowing how to feed the spirit, we try to muffle

its demands in distractions. Mechanically, we have gained in the last generation, but spiritually we have unwittingly lost. The art and craft of housework has diminished but much of the time-consuming drudgery remains. In housework, as in the rest of life, the curtain of mechanization has come down between the mind and the hand.

The church, too, has always been a great centering force for women, more needed than ever before. But are those who attend as ready to give themselves or to receive its message as they used to be? Our daily life does not prepare us for contemplation. How can a single weekly hour of church, helpful as it may be, counteract the many daily hours of distraction that surround us? If we had our contemplative hour at home we might be readier to give ourselves at church and find ourselves more completely renewed. For the need for renewal is still there.

The answer is not in going back, in putting woman in the home and giving her the broom and the needle again. But neither is the answer in dissipating our time and energy in more purposeless occupations, more accumulations which supposedly simplify life but actually burden it, more possessions which we have not the time to use or appreciate, more diversions to fill up the void.

In other words, the answer is not in the feverish pursuit of centrifugal activities which only lead in the end to fragmentation. On the contrary, woman must consciously encourage those pursuits which oppose the centrifugal forces of today. Quiet time alone, contemplation, prayer, music, a centering line of thought or reading, of study or work. It can be physical or intellectual or artistic, any creative life proceeding from oneself. It need not be an enormous project or a great work. But it should be something of one's own. What matters is that one be for a time inwardly attentive.

Solitude, says the moon shell. To the possession of the self the way is inward, says Plotinus. And woman must be the pioneer in this turning inward for strength. But in our recent efforts to emancipate ourselves, to prove ourselves the equal of man, we have been drawn into competing with him in his outward activities, to the neglect of our own inner springs.

Why have we been seduced into abandoning this timeless inner strength of woman for the temporal strength of man? The outer strength of man is essential to the pattern, but even here the reign of purely outer strength and purely outward solutions seems to be waning today. Men, too, are being forced to look inward—to find inner solutions as well as outer ones. Can it be that he is beginning to realize that the kingdom of heaven is within?

Moon shell, who named you? Some intuitive woman, I like to think. You will sit there and fasten your single eye upon me. You will say to me, "solitude," and you will remind me that a woman must be still as the axis of a wheel in the midst of her activities for the salvation of family life, of society, perhaps even of our civilization.

DOUBLE SUNRISE

This shell was a gift; I did not find it. It was handed to me by a friend. It is unusual on the island. Each side, like the wing of a butterfly, is marked with the same pattern; translucent white, except for three rosy rays that fan out from the golden hinge binding the two together. I hold two sunrises between my thumb and finger.

It is unusual; yet it was given to me freely. People are like that here. Strangers smile at you on the beach, come up and offer you a shell, for no reason, and then go by and leave you alone again. Nothing is demanded of you in payment, no social rite expected, no tie established.

The pure relationship, how beautiful it is! How easily it is damaged, or weighed down with irrelevancies—not even irrelevancies, just life itself, the accumulations of life and of time. For the first part of every relationship is pure, whether it be with friend or lover, husband or child.

And then how swiftly, how inevitably the perfect unity is invaded; the relationship changes; it becomes complicated, encumbered by its contact with the world. And it is the marriage relationship in which the changing pattern is shown up most clearly because it is the deepest one and the most arduous to maintain.

It is true, of course, the original relationship is very beautiful. Like its parallel in physical passion, the early ecstatic stage of a relationship cannot continue always at the same pitch of intensity. It moves to another phase of growth which one should not dread, but welcome as one welcomes summer after spring. But there is also an accumulation, a coating of false values, habits, and burdens which blights life. It is this smothering coat that needs constantly to be stripped off, in life as well as in relationships.

Both men and women feel the change in the early relationship and hunger nostalgically for its original pattern as life goes on and becomes more complicated. For inevitably, as the relationship grows, both men and women, at least to some degree, are drawn into their more specialized and functional roles: man, into his less personal work; woman, into her obligations with family and household.

But though both men and women are absorbed in these roles and each misses something of the early relationship, there are great differences in their needs. While man has less chance for personal relations than woman, he may have more opportunity for giving himself creatively in work. Woman, on the other hand, has more chance for personal relations, but these do not give her a sense of creative identity, the individual who has something of her own to say or to give. The temptation is to blame the situation on the other person and to accept the easy solution that a new and more understanding partner will solve everything.

But neither woman nor man is likely to be fed by another relationship which seems easier because it is in an earlier stage. Such a love affair cannot really bring back a sense of identity. Certainly, one has the illusion that one will find oneself in being loved for what one really is, not for a collection of functions. But can one actually find oneself in someone else? Can the pure relationship of the sunrise shell be refound once it has become obscured?

Obviously some relationships can never be recovered. In their changing roles the two

partners may have grown in different directions or at different rates of speed. A brief double-sunrise episode may have been all they could achieve. In a growing relationship, however, the original essence is not lost but merely buried under the impediments of life.

One way of rediscovering the double-sunrise is to duplicate some of its circumstances. Husband and wife can and should go off on vacations alone and also on vacations alone *together*. For if it is possible that woman can find herself by having a vacation alone, it is equally possible that the original relationship can sometimes be refound by having a vacation alone *together*. Most married couples have found the unexpected joy of one of these vacations.

Actually, I believe this temporary return to the pure relationship holds good for one's children, too. If only, I think, playing with my sunrise shell—if only we could have each of our children alone, not just for part of each day, but for part of each month, each year. Would he not be happier, stronger and, in the end, more secure? Does each child not secretly long for the pure relationship he once had with the mother, when he was "The Baby?"

We all wish to be loved alone. But the desire for being continuously loved alone seems to me "the error bred in the bone of man." For, as a friend of mine once said, there is no one-and-only; there are just one-and-only moments.

The one-and-only moments are justified. Even a temporary return to them is valid. Finding shells together, polishing chestnuts, sharing one's treasures — all these moments of together-aloneness are valid, but not permanent.

One comes to realize that there is no permanent pure relationship and there should not be. It is not even something to be desired. The pure relationship is limited, in space and in time. In its essence it implies exclusion. It excludes the rest of life, other relationships, other sides of personality, other responsibilities, other possibilities in the future. The race on the beach together renews one's youth like a dip in the sea. But we are no longer children; life is not a beach. There is no pattern here for permanent return, only for refreshment.

One learns to accept the fact that no perma-

31

nent return is possible to an old form of relationship; and, more deeply still, that there is no holding of a relationship to a single form. This is not tragedy but part of the ever-recurrent miracle of life and growth. All living relationships are in process of change, of expansion, and must perpetually be building themselves new forms.

Beautiful, fragile, fleeting, the sunrise shell; but not, for all that, illusory. Because it is not lasting, let us not fall into the cynic's trap and call it an illusion. Duration is not a test of true and false. Validity need have no relation to time, to duration, to continuity. It is on another plane, judged by other standards. It relates to the actual moment in time and place. The sunrise shell has the eternal validity of all beautiful and fleeting things.

But surely we *do* demand duration and continuity of relationships, at least of marriage. That is what marriage is, isn't it—continuity of relationship? Of course, but not necessarily continuity in one single form or stage.

There are other shells to help me. Here is one I picked up yesterday. Not rare; there are many of them on the beach and yet each one is individual. Each is fitted and formed by its own struggle to survive. It is an oyster.

Sprawling and uneven, it has the irregularity of something growing. It looks rather like the house of a big family, pushing out one addition after another to hold its teeming life— here a sleeping porch, there a veranda; here a garage and there a shed. Like my life at the moment, like most women's lives in the middle years of marriage, it is untidy, spread out in all directions, heavily encrusted with accumulations and, in its living state, firmly imbedded on its rock.

Yes, the oyster shell expresses well the middle years of marriage. It suggests the struggle of life itself. The oyster fought to have its place on the rock to which it clings tenaciously. So most couples in the growing years of marriage struggle to achieve a place in the world. It is a physical and material battle for a place in society, and in the midst of such a life there is not much time to sit facing one another over a breakfast table. In the midst of such a life, one recognizes the truth of Saint-Exupéry's, "Love does not consist of gazing at each other, but in looking outward together in the same direction."

In fact, man and woman are not only *looking* outward in the same direction, they are *working* outward. Here the bonds of marriage are formed; many bonds, many strands, making up a web that is taut and firm. The web of marriage is made by propinquity, in day-to-day living side by side, looking outward and working outward. It is woven in space and in time of the substance of life itself.

But the bond of romantic love is something else. It is the bond of romantic love which fastens the double-sunrise shell, only one bond, one hinge. And if that fragile link is snapped in the storm, what will hold the halves to each other? In the oyster stage of marriage, romantic love is only one of the many bonds that make up the intricate and enduring web that two people have built together.

I am very fond of the oyster shell. It is humble and awkward and ugly. I make fun of its knobbiness. Sometimes I resent its burdens and excrescences. But its tireless adaptability and tenacity draw my astonished admiration and sometimes even my tears.

But is it the permanent symbol of marriage? Should it—any more than the double-sunrise shell—last forever? Most people by middle age have attained, or ceased to struggle to attain, their place in the world. Many of the physical struggles have ceased, due either to success or failure. Does the shell need to be so welded to its rock? What is one to do—die of atrophy in an outstripped form? Or move on to another form, other experiences?

Someone might suggest that this is the moment to go back to the simple self-enclosed world of the sunrise shell. But one cannot go back to that tightly closed world. One has grown too big, too many-sided, for that rigidly symmetrical shell. I am not sure that one has not grown too big for any shell at all.

Perhaps middle age is, or should be, a period of shedding shells; the shell of ambition, the shell of material possessions, the shell of the ego. Perhaps one can shed at this stage in life as one sheds in beach living; one's pride, one's false ambitions, one's mask, one's armor. Was that armor not put on to protect one from the competitive world? If one ceases to compete, does one need it? Perhaps one can at last in middle age, if not earlier, be completely oneself. And what a liberation that would be!

It is true that the adventures of youth are less open to us. Many of the physical, material, and worldly ambitions are less attainable than they were twenty years ago. But is this not often a relief?

The primitive, physical, functional pattern of the morning of life before forty or fifty is outlived. But there is still the afternoon opening up, which one can spend in having time at last for those intellectual, cultural, and spiritual activities that were pushed aside in the heat of the race. But in our breathless attempts we often miss the flowering that waits for afternoon.

For is it not true that middle age can be looked upon as a period of second flowering, second growth? It is true that society in general does not help one accept this interpretation of the second half of life and so this period of expanding is often tragically misunderstood. The signs that presage growth, so similar to those in early adolescence: discontent, restlessness, doubt, despair, longing, are interpreted falsely as signs of decay. One takes them seriously as growing pains, following where they lead. One is afraid. Who is not afraid of pure space—that breath-taking empty space of an open door?

But in middle age, because of the false assumption that it is a period of decline, one takes these life signs, paradoxically, as signs of approaching death. Instead of facing them, one runs away; one escapes—into depression, breakdowns, drink, affairs, or frantic, thoughtless, fruitless overwork. Anything, rather than face them. One tries to cure the signs of growth, to exorcise them, when really they might be angels of annunciation.

Angels of annunciation of what? Of a new stage of living when, having shed many of the physical struggles, the worldly ambitions, the material encumbrances of active life, one might be free to fulfill the neglected side of one's self. One might be free for growth of mind, heart, and talent; free at last for spiritual growth; free of the clamping sunrise shell. Beautiful as it was, it was still a closed world one had to outgrow. And the time may come when—comfortable and adaptable as it is—one may outgrow even the oyster shell.

There are in the beach world certain rare creatures, the "Argonauta" (Paper Nautilus), who are not fastened to their shells at all. The shell is actually a cradle for the young, held in the arms of the mother argonaut who floats with it to the surface, where the eggs hatch and the young swim away. Then the mother leaves the shell and starts another life.

I am fascinated by this image, whose temporary dwelling I have seen only as the treasure of a specialist's collection. Almost transparent, delicately fluted like a Greek column, this narcissus-white snail shell is feather-light as some coracle of ancient times, ready to set sail across unknown seas.

Lovely shell, lovely image—I am tempted to play with it in my mind. Is this the symbol for another stage in relationships? Can we middle-aged argonauts, when we outgrow the oyster bed, look forward to the freedom of the nautilus who has left its shell for the open seas? And in this new freedom, is there any place for a relationship?

I believe there is, after the oyster bed, an opportunity for the best relationship of all: not a limited, mutually exclusive one, like the sunrise shell, and not a functional, dependent one, as in the oyster bed; but the meeting of two whole, fully developed people as persons.

But this new relationship of persons as persons, this more human love, this two solitudes conception is not something that comes easily. It must have grown, like all firm-rooted growth, slowly. It cannot be reached until woman—individually and as a sex—has herself come of age, a maturing process we are witnessing today.

And she must come of age by herself. This is the essence of "coming of age"—to learn how to stand alone. She must learn not to depend on another, nor to feel she must prove her strength by competing. She must become whole. She must, as a prelude to any "two solitudes" relationship, follow the advice of the poet to become "world to oneself for another's sake."

In fact, I wonder if both man and woman must not accomplish this heroic feat. Must not man also become a world to himself? Must he not also expand the neglected sides of his per-

sonality; the art of inward looking he has seldom had time for; the personal relationships
he has not had much chance to enjoy; the so-
called feminine qualities, aesthetic, emotion-
al, cultural and spiritual, which he has been
too rushed to fully develop?

This greater wholeness in each person, this
being "world to oneself," does this not mean
greater self-sufficiency and, therefore, inevitably, greater separation between man and
woman? No, for the two separate worlds or
the two solitudes will surely have more to give
each other than when each was a meager half.

This is a beautiful image, but who can achieve
it in actual life? Theory precedes exploration;
we must use any signposts that exist to help
us try to find a new path through the maze of
tradition, convention and dogma. Our efforts
are part of the struggle to mature the conception of relationships between men and
women, and every step, even a tentative one,
counts. And though we may seldom come
upon a perfect argonauta life cycle, we have
all had glimpses of them; and these brief experiences give us insight into what the new
relation might be.

45

A good relationship has a pattern like a dance and is built on some of the same rules. The partners do not need to hold on tightly, because they move in the same pattern, intricate but gay and swift and free, like a country dance. The joy of such a pattern is not only the joy of creation or the joy of participation, it is also the joy of living the moment.

But how does one learn this technique of the dance? Why is it so difficult? What makes us hesitate and stumble? It is fear, I think, that makes one cling nostalgically to the last moment or clutch greedily toward the next. But when the heart is flooded with love there is no room in it for fear, for doubt, for hesitation. And it is this lack of fear that makes for the dance. When each partner loves so completely that he has forgotten to ask himself whether or not he is loved in return; when he only knows that he loves and is moving to its music —then, and then only, are two people able to dance perfectly in tune to the same rhythm.

But should they not also be in tune with a larger rhythm, a natural swinging of the pendulum between sharing and solitude; the intimate and the abstract, the near and the far?

And in this image of the pendulum swinging between opposite poles, is there not a clue to the problem of relationships as a whole? Is there not here a hint of an understanding and acceptance of the eternal ebb and flow and inevitable intermittency of life's relationships?

For the life of our emotions and our relationships is intermittent. When you love someone you do not love them all the time, in exactly the same way, from moment to moment. It is an impossibility. It is even a lie to pretend to. And yet this is exactly what most of us demand. We have so little faith in the ebb and flow of life, of love, of relationships. We leap at the flow of the tide and resist in terror its ebb. We are afraid it will never return. We insist on permanency, on duration, on continuity; when the only continuity possible, in life as in love, is in growth, in fluidity—in freedom, in the sense that the dancers are free, barely touching as they pass, but partners in the same pattern.

Intermittency—an impossible lesson for human beings to learn. How can one learn to live through the ebb tides of one's existence? It is easier to understand here on the beach, where the breathlessly still ebb tides reveal another life below the level which mortals usually reach; one has a revelation of the secret kingdom at the bottom of the sea.

Here one finds, wading through warm ripples, great horse conches, white sand dollars, and myriads of bright-colored cochina clams glistening in the foam. So beautiful is the still hour of the sea's withdrawal.

Perhaps this is the most important thing for me to take back from beach living: simply the memory that each cycle of the tide is valid; each cycle of a relationship is valid. And my shells? I can sweep them all into my pocket. They are only there to remind me that the sea recedes and returns eternally.

I am packing to leave my island. What have I for my efforts, for my ruminations on the beach? What answers or solutions have I found for my life? I have a few shells in my pocket, a few clues, only a few.

When I think back to my first days here, I realize how greedily I collected. My pockets bulged with wet shells. The beach was covered with beautiful shells. I could not let one go by unnoticed. I couldn't even walk head up looking out to sea, for fear of missing something precious at my feet. But after all the pockets were stretched and damp, I began to drop my acquisitiveness. I began to discard from my possessions, to select.

One cannot collect all the beautiful shells on the beach. One can collect only a few, and they are more beautiful if they are few. Gradually one discards and keeps just the perfect specimen. One sets it apart by itself, ringed around by space—like the island.

For it is only framed in space that beauty blooms. Only in space are events and objects and people unique and significant—and therefore beautiful. Even small and casual things take on significance if they are washed in space, like a few autumn grasses in one corner of an Oriental painting, the rest of the page bare.

My life at home, I begin to realize, lacks this quality of significance and therefore of beauty, because there is so little empty space. There are so few empty pages in my engagement pad, too many activities, and people, and things. Too many worthy activities, valuable things, and interesting people. For it is not merely the trivial which clutters our lives but the important as well. We can have a surfeit of treasures—an excess of shells, where one or two would be significant.

But here on this island I have had space. Here there is time; time to be quiet; time to work without pressure; time to think; time to watch the heron; time to look at the stars or to study a shell; time to see friends, to gossip, to laugh, to talk. Time, even, *not* to talk.

At home, when I meet my friends in those cubby-holed hours, time is so precious we feel we must cram every available instant with conversation. We cannot afford the luxury of silence. Here on the island I find I can sit with a friend without talking, sharing the day's last sliver of pale green light on the horizon, or the whorls in a small white shell, or the dark scar left in a dazzling night sky by a shooting star. Then communication becomes communion and one is nourished as one never is by words.

Island living selects for me, but it is a natural, not an artificial selection. It selects numerically but not in kind; there are all kinds of experiences on an island, but not too many.

There are all kinds of people, but not too many. The simplicity of life forces me into physical as well as intellectual or social activity. I have no car, so I bicycle for my supplies and my mail. When it is cold, I collect driftwood for my fireplace and chop it up, too. I swim instead of taking hot baths. I bury my garbage instead of having it removed by truck. And when I cannot write a poem, I bake biscuits and feel just as pleased. Most of these physical chores would be burdens at home, where my life is crowded and schedules are tight. There I have a house full of children and I am responsible for many people's lives. Here, where there is time and space, the physical

tasks are a welcome change. They balance my life in a way I find refreshing and in which I seldom feel refreshed at home. Making beds or driving to market is not as refreshing as swimming or bicycling or digging in the earth. I cannot go on burying the garbage when I get home, but I can dig in a garden; I can bicycle to the cabin where I work; and I can remember to bake biscuits on bad days.

My island selects for me socially too. Its small circumference cannot hold too many people. I see people here that I would not see at home, people who are removed from me by age or occupation. In the suburbs of a large city we tend to see people of the same general age and interests. That is why we chose the suburbs, because we have similar needs and pursuits. My island selects for me people who are very different from me—the stranger who turns out to be, in the frame of sufficient time and space, invariably interesting and enriching. I discover here what everyone has experienced on an ocean voyage or a long train ride or a temporary seclusion in a small village. Out of the welter of life, a few people are selected for us by the accident of temporary confinement in the same circle. We never would have chosen these neighbors; life chose them for us. But thrown together on this island of living, we stretch to understand each other and are invigorated by the stretching.

The difficulty with big city environment is that we tend to select people like ourselves, a very monotonous diet. We tend not to choose the unknown which might be a shock or a disappointment or simply a little difficult to cope with. And yet it is the unknown with all its disappointments and surprises that is the most enriching.

In so many ways this island selects for me better than I do myself at home. When I go back will I be submerged again not only by distractions but by too many opportunities? Not only by dull people but by too many interesting ones? The multiplicity of the world will crowd in on me again with its false sense of values. Values weighed in quantity, not quality; in speed, not stillness; in noise, not silence; in words, not in thoughts; in acquisitiveness, not beauty. How shall I resist the onslaught? How shall I remain whole against these stresses and strains?

For the natural selectivity of the island I have

to substitute a conscious selectivity based on another sense of values—a sense of values I have become more aware of here. Island-precepts, I might call them if I could define them, signposts toward another way of living. Simplicity of living, as much as possible, to retain a true awareness of life. Balance of physical, intellectual, and spiritual life. Work without pressure. Space for significance and beauty. Time for solitude and sharing. Closeness to nature to strengthen understanding and faith in the intermittency of life: life of the spirit, creative life, and the life of human relationships. A few shells.

Island living has been a lens through which to examine my own life in the North. I must keep my lens when I go back. Little by little one's holiday vision tends to fade. I must remember to see with island eyes. The shells will remind me; they must be my island eyes.

I pick up my sisal bag. The sand slips softly under my feet. The time for reflection is almost over.

The search for outward simplicity, for inner integrity, for fuller relationship—is this not a limited outlook? Today, a kind of planetal point of view has burst upon mankind. We are asked today to feel compassionately for everyone in the world; to digest all the information spread out in public print; and to implement in action every ethical impulse aroused by our hearts and minds.

Our grandmothers, and even our mothers, lived in a circle small enough to let them implement in action most of the impulses of their hearts and minds. But we are brought up in a tradition that has now become impossible, for we have extended our circle throughout space and time.

Faced with this dilemma, what can we do? We are forced to make a compromise. Because we cannot deal with the many as individuals, we sometimes try to simplify the many into an abstraction called the mass. But can one really feel deeply for an abstraction called a mass? Can one make the future a substitute for the present? And what guarantee have we that the future will be any better if we neglect the present? Can one solve world problems when one is unable to solve one's own?

If we stop to think about it, are not the real casualties in modern life the now, the individual and his relationships? The present is passed over in the race for the future; the here is neglected in favor of the there; and the individual is dwarfed by the enormity of the mass.

The good past is so far away and the near past is so horrible and the future is so perilous, that the present has a chance to expand into a golden eternity of here and now. Perhaps we never appreciate the here and now until it is challenged, as it is beginning to be today, even in America.

The here, the now, and the individual have always been the special concern of woman. In the small circle of the home she has never quite forgotten the particular uniqueness of each member of the family; the spontaneity of now; the vividness of here. This is the basic substance of life. We may neglect these ele-

ments, but we cannot dispense with them. They are the drops that make up the stream. They are the essence of life itself.

When we start at the center of ourselves, we discover something worthwhile extending toward the periphery of the circle. We find again some of the joy in the now, some of the peace in the here, some of the love in me and thee which go to make up the kingdom of heaven on earth.

The waves echo behind me. Patience—Faith—Openness, is what the sea has to teach. Simplicity—Solitude—Intermittency . . . But there are other beaches to explore. There are more shells to find. This is only a beginning.

Set at The Castle Press in Intertype Walbaum,
a light, open typeface designed by Justus
Erich Walbaum (1768-1839), who was a type
founder at Goslar and at Weimar.
Printed on Hallmark Eggshell Book paper.
Designed by Harald Peter.